PORCELAIN

by Margaret Perry

║SAMUEL FRENCH║

samuelfrench.co.uk

Copyright © 2018 by Margaret Perry
All Rights Reserved

PORCELAIN is fully protected under the copyright laws of the British Commonwealth, including Canada, the United States of America, and all other countries of the Copyright Union. All rights, including professional and amateur stage productions, recitation, lecturing, public reading, motion picture, radio broadcasting, television and the rights of translation into foreign languages are strictly reserved.

ISBN 978-0-573-11533-2

www.samuelfrench.co.uk
www.samuelfrench.com

FOR AMATEUR PRODUCTION ENQUIRIES

UNITED KINGDOM AND WORLD
EXCLUDING NORTH AMERICA
plays@samuelfrench.co.uk
020 7255 4302/01

Each title is subject to availability from Samuel French, depending upon country of performance.

CAUTION: Professional and amateur producers are hereby warned that *PORCELAIN* is subject to a licensing fee. Publication of this play does not imply availability for performance. Both amateurs and professionals considering a production are strongly advised to apply to the appropriate agent before starting rehearsals, advertising, or booking a theatre. A licensing fee must be paid whether the title is presented for charity or gain and whether or not admission is charged.

The professional rights in this play are controlled by Samuel French Ltd, 24-32 Stephenson Way, London NW1 2HD.

No one shall make any changes in this title for the purpose of production. No part of this book may be reproduced, stored in a retrieval system, or transmitted in any form, by any means, now known or yet to be invented, including mechanical, electronic, photocopying, recording, videotaping, or otherwise, without the prior written permission of the publisher. No one shall upload this title, or part of this title, to any social media websites.

The right of Margaret Perry to be identified as author of this work has been asserted in accordance with Section 77 of the Copyright, Designs and Patents Act 1988.

THINKING ABOUT PERFORMING A SHOW?

There are thousands of plays and musicals available to perform from Samuel French right now, and applying for a licence is easier and more affordable than you might think

From classic plays to brand new musicals, from monologues to epic dramas, there are shows for everyone.

Plays and musicals are protected by copyright law so if you want to perform them, the first thing you'll need is a licence. This simple process helps support the playwright by ensuring they get paid for their work, and means that you'll have the documents you need to stage the show in public.

Not all our shows are available to perform all the time, so it's important to check and apply for a licence before you start rehearsals or commit to doing the show.

LEARN MORE & FIND THOUSANDS OF SHOWS

Browse our full range of plays and musicals and find out more about how to license a show

www.samuelfrench.co.uk/perform

Talk to the friendly experts in our Licensing team for advice on choosing a show, and help with licensing

plays@samuelfrench.co.uk   020 7387 9373

Acting Editions
BORN TO PERFORM

Playscripts designed from the ground up to work the way you do in rehearsal, performance and study

Larger, clearer text for easier reading

Wider margins for notes

Performance features such as character and props lists, sound and lighting cues, and more

+ CHOOSE A SIZE AND STYLE TO SUIT YOU

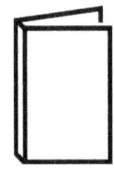

STANDARD EDITION

Our regular paperback book at our regular size

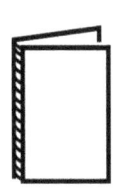

SPIRAL-BOUND EDITION

The same size as the Standard Edition, but with a sturdy, easy-to-fold, easy-to-hold spiral-bound spine

LARGE EDITION

A4 size and spiral bound, with larger text and a blank page for notes opposite every page of text. Perfect for technical and directing use

| LEARN MORE | samuelfrench.co.uk/actingeditions

Porcelain premiered at the Abbey Theatre, Dublin on 16 February 2018 with the following cast (in alphabetical order):

Bill	Bamshad Abedi-Amin
Sarah	Caitríona Ennis
Michael Cleary	Keith McErlean
Silvertongue	Helen Norton
Bridget Cleary	Toni O'Rourke
Hat	Lola Petticrew

PRODUCTION CREDITS

Written by	Margaret Perry
Directed by	Cathal Cleary
Set and Costumer Designer	Cécile Trémolières
Lighting Designer	Paul Keogan
Composer and Sound Designer	Denis Clohessy
Casting	Amy Rowan
Dramaturgy	Jesse Weaver
Hair and Make Up	Val Sherlock
Voice Director	Andrea Ainsworth
Production Manager	Cliff Barragry
Stage Manager	Diarmuid O'Quigley
Deputy Stage Manager	Anne Kyle
Set Builder	Ian Thompson
Scenic Artist	Liz Barker
Sign Language Interpreter	Ali Stewart
Graphic Design	Zoo

ABOUT THE AUTHOR

Margaret Perry is a playwright from Cork. She has a BA in Drama and Theatre Studies from University College Cork, an MA in Dramatic Writing from Central St Martins and she spent a year studying creative writing on a scholarship at the University of California, Berkeley. Her previous plays include *Goose Chase* (Granary Theatre), *Icarus* (Theatre Upstairs/Bunker Theatre), *Turf* (Kings Head Theatre) and *Collapsible* (The Miniaturists/MGC Futures bursary). *Porcelain* is her debut at the Abbey Theatre, and her first professional production. She lives in London.

To my parents, Mary and Ivan. Without your unwavering love and support I don't think I'd be here.

THANK YOUS

To Graham, Neil, Jen, Cathal, Paddy Jo and everyone at the Abbey – thank you from the bottom of my heart for believing in *Porcelain* and taking a chance on me. Special thanks to Jesse Weaver for his incredible dramaturgy and support throughout this process. A huge thank you to the many people who encouraged me and this play along its journey, particularly Deirdre O'Halloran at the Soho Theatre and Catriona Craig at Out of Joint, and to my brilliant friend Maud Dromgoole for our many fruitful conversations about the script. Finally, thank you to my amazing family and friends who've come from Cork, Sligo, London and further afield to see the show. I'm so lucky to have you all in my corner.

The Burning of Bridget Cleary: A True Story by Angela Bourke was an invaluable resource in researching the lives of Bridget and Michael Cleary.

CHARACTERS

HAT – F, twenty-six, Irish
BILL – M, Hat's boyfriend, a Londoner
SARAH – F, Hat's cousin, Irish, a little younger than Hat
SILVERTONGUE – any gender, any age, a shapeshifter
BRIDGET – F, twenty-six, Irish
An imagining of Bridget Cleary
MICHAEL – M, Bridget's husband, Irish
An imagining of Michael Cleary
JOY – Hat and Bill's baby, represented by anything that can be cradled.

SETTING

London and Tipperary, 1895 and now. Part of the stage is a slick, modern space, devoid of personality and full of hard shiny surfaces. Another part is the suggestion of an Irish country kitchen at the turn of the twentieth century. These playing areas should not be rigidly bordered but layer over and bleed into one another. Likewise, Hat's and Bridget's scenes, and their physical worlds, should overlap wherever possible.

AUTHOR'S NOTE

A character's name followed by a blank, eg. (HAT   ) indicates a non-verbal response.

1. Starbucks

London, 2017.

SARAH, in a Starbucks, waiting. HAT enters, wearing a coat and wheeling baby JOY in a buggy. If HAT is cloud, SARAH is earth.

SARAH Hi.

HAT Hello.

SARAH *(gesturing to a huge foamy creamy drink with an unintelligible name scrawled across it)* Got you a – this.

HAT takes the drink and slurps it. Then gulps it. Her hands tremble.

You didn't need to come out. I could have come to the house—

HAT Didn't want to do it in my house. Didn't want to do it somewhere I have to be again, ever in my life.

SARAH I was wondering why you picked here.

HAT *(viciously)* You'd have preferred somewhere trendier? Somewhere with more exposed wood and – beards?

SARAH No – I'm sorry – I didn't mean to –

Pause.

The coffee's shit, is all.

Pause.

HAT No. I'm sorry. Don't you be sorry. Don't be sorry are you stupid, you're saving me.

SARAH Do you think?

HAT I know you are.

SARAH Because I've been worrying—

HAT Don't worry.

SARAH I've just been thinking—

HAT Don't think about it.

SARAH Have you? Thought about it?

HAT Of course I have. Of course I have Sarah all I've done is think all day all night it's all I've been thinking about.

Pause.

SARAH You'll change your mind.

HAT I won't.

SARAH How do you know?

HAT I wouldn't do that to you.

Pause.

SARAH It's not as simple as this.

HAT It is.

SARAH There's a formal process, Hat, a lot of things to sign.

HAT Find out. You find out and show me where I.

Pause.

SARAH You'll always be welcome. You know that don't you. To come and...

Pause.

That goes without saying really. I think. I'm not sure but I think that should go without saying.

Pause.

What about Bill?

HAT He's been his usual. My walking safety net.

Pause.

SARAH And he thinks, this is the best thing.

HAT He just wants me to be happy.

SARAH Okay. Okay.

HAT It's not like you're a stranger.

Pause.

SARAH When we were kids – never thought what could happen did we. Never ever thought this/

HAT /You remember the Little Princess? Practising that bit where she finds her dad, over and over/

SARAH /running into your arms in the rain.

HAT Rubbing your snotty face all over me.

SARAH I was always crying wasn't I.

HAT I remember.

SARAH I liked it. The intensity of it.

Pause.

You hardly ever cried.

Pause.

HAT I'm sorry I've not been better at keeping in touch. I should have – when you –

Pause.

I should have called you.

SARAH You'd be surprised how few people actually I mean how many people just said nothing. Just acted like I'd never been pregnant at all, I mean it's not like a real – death you know of a – a whole, person/

HAT /when you moved here, this city can feel so lonely and I should have/

SARAH /It was me too. I haven't really been – I mean I didn't know how to—

Pause.

We're not friends really. Why would we stay in touch? We got shoved together growing up because we're girls and we're the same age but we never really –

HAT Mum and Auntie Claire were determined we would be best friends.

SARAH You were so chatty. I felt like a shy lump whenever you came to visit.

Pause.

HAT I remember when we were kids you said that this was your dream. I remember I sneered at you in my mind. What a small ambition. Anyone can do that. But they can't. I. Know now that they can't.

Pause.

SARAH This is so strange. Just the strangest thing I have ever—

HAT *almost might vomit.*

HAT I need to go.

SARAH Okay.

HAT *just sits there.*

HAT I'm going to go.

SARAH Alright.

HAT *gets up. She does not look into the buggy.*

I'll call you.

HAT Don't.

SARAH I'll call you, check in on you/

HAT /Don't. Please, Sarah.

Pause.

SARAH You have my number.

HAT *tries to say something else, a parting word. She can't. She goes, leaving the buggy behind.* **SARAH** *puts her hand into the buggy, bends over the baby.*

Hello.

A kind of light in her eyes. Then she goes too, in a different direction, pushing the buggy.

2. Walking

Tipperary, 1895. **BRIDGET**'s *wearing muddy wellies.*

MICHAEL Cá raibh tú? (*Where were you?*)

BRIDGET Amuigh ag siúl. (*Walking.*)

MICHAEL Cé leis? (*Who with?*)

BRIDGET M'anonar. (*Alone.*)

MICHAEL I'd have come with you.

Pause.

I'd have come, if you'd said.

Pause.

The back of your dress is wet.

BRIDGET I lay in the grass for a while.

3. Congratulations

Tipperary, 2016. **HAT**'s *got a pint in front of her.* **SARAH**'s *having an orange juice.*

HAT You changed your hair.

SARAH About a year ago.

HAT Oh.

Pause.

It's nice.

SARAH Thanks.

Pause.

So!

HAT So!

SARAH So I hear congratulations are in order!

HAT Yeah. I'm off tomorrow.

SARAH Mum said. London, no less! That's great news. All your hard work and studying finally paying off!

HAT Yeah, well/

SARAH /All those masters degrees.

HAT Just the one.

SARAH Are you sure? I thought you had more.

HAT No.

SARAH Just feels like you've been a student forever.

Pause.

Well sure look, it paid off!

HAT Well it's an admin job. So not exactly what I studied – but it's a start.

SARAH That's so great. I'm so pleased for you.

HAT Can't wait to get out of here.

Pause.

SARAH Kieran and I are buying a house here actually.

HAT Wow. Well this is a – lovely peaceful place to live.

SARAH I'm sure you'll make a splash in London.

They smile at each other for just a little bit too long.
SARAH *rather pointedly sips her orange juice.*

HAT Oh my God, I can't believe I haven't said yet – I heard your news as well, you look great!

SARAH I'm not showing as much as I had hoped.

HAT Is that bad?

SARAH It's stupid but I'd hoped to have that thing where strangers come up to me in the street and ask to feel my belly? You know? But people just think I'm chubby.

HAT No. You look great.

SARAH I don't really.

HAT You do.

SARAH Thanks. But I don't.

HAT You really do.

SARAH Thank you. You don't mean that.

Pause.

HAT How is Kieran?

SARAH Overjoyed.

3. CONGRATULATIONS

HAT Good.

SARAH I really wanted him to join us but he's working some extra hours to save some cash for the baby.

HAT I hear babies usually want to head to Vegas and play the slots pretty much as soon as they're born. That's just what I've heard.

Pause.

SARAH It's more for safety stuff, like a really secure buggy and car seat.

HAT I know, I was just. Joking.

SARAH Oh! I forgot that you do that.

HAT Yeah.

SARAH It has been a while. Hasn't it.

HAT Yonks.

Pause.

SARAH So how's your love life?

HAT

SARAH What! I just want to know.

HAT I have a beautiful lover. He will wave his perfectly-ironed handkerchief out of the terminal window and shed a single tear as I board my one-way Ryanair flight.

SARAH Hat.

HAT What.

SARAH I don't know why I bother.

HAT There's nobody.

SARAH Oh.

HAT Sorry to disappoint.

Pause.

SARAH It is great, being single though! I used to make myself a mojito of an evening and just sit on my own for hours.

HAT Yeah?

SARAH It was amazing. The quiet.

HAT I can't tell if you're joking.

SARAH What do you mean?

HAT Never mind.

SARAH I love mojitos. Obviously I love Kieran more though.

HAT Obviously. A mojito can't pick out a car seat.

Pause.

SARAH You're bound to meet a handsome English man.

HAT I might. I might not.

SARAH You're bound to.

HAT I pray for it every night.

Pause.

Listen, you'll have to come visit. Kieran too, and the baby—

SARAH We will, of course, when she's big enough.

HAT She?

SARAH Having a girl. Didn't I tell you? We're having a girl.

HAT Sarah – oh that's amazing. Come here.

She embraces her. A genuine moment.

SARAH You can show her all the sights. Lift her up to look out over the bridges.

HAT I'd love that. You could even stay with me – I mean I don't know where I'll be living yet so it might be a dump but you'd be welcome.

SARAH You're just saying that.

HAT I mean it. Seriously.

SARAH Thank you.

They smile at one another, more warmly this time.

HAT Crazy to think this time tomorrow I'll be there. I get to walk past one of my favourite paintings in the whole world on my way to my office, I can't believe it. Do you want to see?

SARAH Sure.

HAT *takes out her phone and shows* **SARAH**, *the screen a square of light.* **SARAH** *politely looks at it.*

HAT I mean you can look at something on Google Images all you like but it's just a copy. Just *empty* compared to standing in front of the real thing, you know what I mean?

Pause.

SARAH What time's your flight?

4. Gold

Tipperary, 1895.

BRIDGET's *working at the kitchen table. Her feet are bare, her muddy boots beside her. She's cutting fabric into panels to make a skirt. The fabric is grey. She's engrossed and enjoying the rhythm of cutting and giving shape to the material. After she's cut it up, she reaches underneath it and pulls out a small square of gold silk she's been hoarding. She holds it up to the light, and smiles a private smile.*

5. Out on a Limb

London, 2016.

HAT *and* **BILL**, *at a work party. They are both a bit drunk.* **BILL** *is holding a plate of canapés and methodically eating his way through them.* **HAT**'s *watching.* **BILL** *realises he's not alone.*

BILL Didn't have dinner, so—

HAT No judgement over here.

BILL Hello.

HAT Hello.

BILL Hi.

HAT Do I know you?

BILL Don't think so.

HAT Good. Even though I've lived here a while now I still have that raised-in-a-small-town fear that I have actually met everyone already and forgotten their names.

BILL Bill.

HAT Hat.

BILL What?

HAT Hat. Like a hat.

BILL Is it short for something?

HAT No.

BILL Cool. It's a cool name.

HAT Thanks.

Pause.

Is yours short for something?

BILL William.

HAT Standard.

Pause.

When I picture a Bill, I picture a man who buys ties in packs of three.

BILL They're cheaper in bulk.

HAT *grins at him.*

So, what department do you work in?

HAT Oh I'm King of Administrative Services.

Pause.

That is my official title.

BILL Right.

HAT Can we skip this bit, would you mind.

BILL What?

HAT Just this is the boring bit and I wonder if we need to go through it.

Pause.

What do you think?

BILL

HAT We can if you want, what do you do, oh you do that, that's an interesting thing which vaguely resembles the thing that I do—

BILL You are frighteningly confident.

HAT I'm actually terrified, standing out here on this limb.

BILL And hugely presumptuous.

5. OUT ON A LIMB

HAT Standing out here on this twig, basically it's actually a tiny flimsy twig and I'm going to fall to my death any second—

He kisses her.

BILL Was that

HAT Yep.

BILL I don't normally

HAT *(with gravitas)* You're the sexiest Bill I've ever met.

BILL Thank you?

She laughs.

HAT I'm going to go and get my coat. Alright?

BILL Yes.

HAT Okay then.

She goes.

BILL *(to himself)* Fuck.

A smile envelops his whole face.

6. Drenched

Tipperary, 1895.

The light sound of rain. **BRIDGET***'s trying on the skirt that she's made. It's long and grey but it fits well and she feels good in it. She swishes it a little, then slyly, like she's surprising herself, she turns up the hem. The square of gold silk is sewn there. She drops her hem as* **MICHAEL** *enters, water on his shoulders and in his hair.*

MICHAEL Will it ever let up.

She moves to greet him.

I'd like to sit out for a bit if it'd let up.

BRIDGET That'd be nice.

She helps him take off his coat.

MICHAEL Sit out with you. Make the most of this view.

Pause.

What are you thinking about?

Pause.

BRIDGET The washing. It'll be drenched.

Pause.

MICHAEL Wouldn't I love to climb inside your mind and take a look around.

She goes.

7. Good Reviews

London, 2016.

HAT *and* **BILL** *sit across from each other, midway through a meal. On the other side of the stage,* **BRIDGET** *stands in the rain, unpegging a white sheet languorously, getting drenched. She turns her face upwards to feel the rain fall. At some point before the end of the scene, she goes inside.*

BILL It's nice to get out. Isn't it?

HAT Yes.

BILL Is your food nice?

HAT Yeah.

BILL Is your wine nice?

HAT Very.

Pause.

BILL Do you like this place?

HAT It's lovely.

BILL It had good reviews.

HAT I know. I said it's lovely.

BILL Okay.

Pause.

I just want you to enjoy yourself.

HAT I am.

Pause.

BILL It doesn't seem like you are.

HAT Well you demanding that I enjoy myself isn't going to make me enjoy myself more.

BILL I just want you to be happy.

HAT I know.

BILL Do you love me?

HAT Yes.

BILL I love you.

HAT I know.

BILL What's wrong then?

HAT Nothing's wrong.

8. Haircut

London, 2017.

HAT sitting facing out. An **ENGLISH HAIRDRESSER** *stands behind her. It's the actor playing* **SILVERTONGUE**.

HAIRDRESSER Brought you some magazines people like magazines usually don't they.

HAT I'm alright.

HAIRDRESSER Have one will you. Good to read about what to wear how to wear it what to say while you're wearing it, very useful information and it relieves the pressure to talk to one another, doesn't it, in this peculiar intimate situation where you've paid me to touch your head.

Pause. **HAT** *takes a magazine.*

HAT Thanks.

She spreads it on her lap and starts to flick through it. The **HAIRDRESSER** *takes out a large pair of scissors and starts to check the length of* **HAT**'s *hair.*

HAIRDRESSER Chin up. Very long isn't it it's very long. You going anywhere special?

HAT Going home. For a wedding.

HAIRDRESSER Oh lovely isn't that lovely back to—

HAT Ireland.

HAIRDRESSER Back to Ireland that's lovely isn't it.

Pause.

HAT They've not seen me since I moved here. I want to look different, you know? More – I dunno. Just totally different.

HAIRDRESSER You're sure then? It's a big change an awfully big change really most people do it more gradually, cut a bit and then come back and cut a bit more that's sort of if you like the more standard way to do it and also I get more money that way.

HAT I'm sure.

HAIRDRESSER You know I can't glue it back on don't you. You understand I can't sew it back on or sit it down and have a little chat with it and persuade it to go back on.

HAT I know.

HAIRDRESSER Okay. On your head be it.

The **HAIRDRESSER** *chops off all of* **HAT**'s *hair.* **HAT** *looks at herself. She touches her head.*

9. Quiet

Tipperary, 1895.

BRIDGET*'s washing dishes, looking out the window.* **MICHAEL***'s at the kitchen table. The sloshing sound of the dishwater is like the sea.*

MICHAEL You're very quiet tonight.

Pause.

Some people's wives'd be nothing but chat. Some people I could think of, you know, their houses are brimful of chat, they find themselves slipping on it on the stairs and catching it in the drain in the sink. Sweeping it out from the kitchen corners and finding it in a dusty layer on the mantelpiece. Feeling it lumpy in the pillow where they lay their heads.

Pause.

Not in this house.

Pause. **BRIDGET** *inhales.*

10. Fort

Tipperary, 2017.

HAT *and* **BILL** *stand, dressed for weather.*

BILL There's something in the air here.

HAT Cow shit. That would be cow shit.

BILL No it's – really peaceful.

HAT It's just some stones in a circle really.

BILL I think it's beautiful.

Pause.

Let's sit for a bit.

He does, and beckons **HAT** *to join him. She rests her head on his shoulder.*

How am I doing?

HAT Very well.

BILL You've got so many uncles. I've never seen that many uncles in one room before.

HAT Well, word on the uncle grapevine is you're a hit.

BILL Oh I'm so glad.

HAT You could probably go easy on the local knowledge though?

BILL Too much?

HAT You sound like a travel guide.

BILL Probably like the one I read on the plane.

HAT That explains a lot.

BILL I wanted to be prepared for this.

Pause.

Your dad's quite frightening.

HAT He means well he's just – set in his ways. Sort of poured concrete levels of set so it can be difficult to get through to him. But I really think that he likes you.

Pause.

It means a lot to me that you came. That you're making such an effort.

BILL I wouldn't have missed it.

Pause. Tender.

Hat?

HAT Mm?

BILL You said you wanted to talk?

Pause.

HAT Do you know the story of this place then?

BILL "A ringfort, believed to be a fairy dwelling-place."

HAT That all it says in the guide?

BILL There's only two pages on the whole of Tipperary to be honest.

HAT See that house over there?

BILL Yeah?

HAT In the late 1800s there was this couple living there. Bridget and Michael Cleary. There's a rhyme about them. Are you a witch, or are you a fairy, or are you the wife of Michael Clare-y?

BILL Is it Clare-y? Or Cleary?

HAT I dunno. That's just how the rhyme goes. Anyway, the village – the village thought the house was cursed because it was so close to the fairy fort. But Bridget and Michael weren't afraid. They got married, moved in. So far so good.

BILL And then they got to have loads of kids and watch each other grow old until they eventually died of natural causes on the same day.

Pause.

HAT Bridget got sick. She couldn't get out of bed, the stories go, and Michael became convinced that she'd been stolen away by the fairies and replaced with a changeling.

BILL A what?

HAT A changeling. He said that she had been swapped for a sort of copy of her. A replica, that looked just like her and sounded just like her. That could fool everyone.

BILL So what happened?

HAT Michael wanted to find out if she was really his wife. So he burned her alive. He burned her alive with her relatives, her aunts and cousins, all watching. He claimed he thought she'd come back to him, once the changeling was gone—

Pause.

BILL Shit.

Pause.

HAT They buried her body near the river, just over there. When they found it she was crouching. Knees drawn up to her chest. *(pause)* I got a bit obsessed with Bridget after that. Read everything about her that I could get my hands on. I used to come here all the time when I was a teenager, and sit on one of the stones in the rain.

BILL Good spot for a brood, I bet.

HAT I was a goth, so.

BILL You weren't.

HAT Oh yeah. Totally.

BILL I can't picture it.

HAT I had so many black lace corsets.

BILL I'm listening.

> **HAT** *laughs. She settles back next to him.*

HAT No it was more that – I liked the idea of a changeling. Of having someone else be you, for a bit. *(pause)* I used to sit here and listen to this ridiculous operatic metal on my Discman and think about her. Say her name, you know, to the grass and the cows. Bridget. *(low and spooky)* Bridget Cleary...

> **BILL** *mock-jumps.* **HAT**'s *nervous.*

BILL What is it?

> *She bites her nails.*

Whatever it is, you can tell me.

HAT This feels, it feels like a weird time to tell you this.

BILL Tell me what?

HAT I should just wait 'til we're back home—

BILL Tell me what.

> *Pause.*

HAT Okay. I guess – I'll just say it.

BILL

HAT I was – late and I didn't say anything to you because I thought it was stress or just nothing or something but actually well I did a test in the loo on the plane and it transpires that I'm pregnant.

BILL

HAT I'm not sure what to do and I wondered what you thought.

BILL

HAT Bill.

Pause.

BILL What do you want to do?

HAT I've been turning it over since I found out and I know what would be the sensible thing to do. Abortion. When we get home, obviously. Get on with our lives but part of me feels like this warmth when I think about it this kind of glowing feeling underneath all my thoughts. And last night I dreamed that my arms were like, full of fruit, which I know is nothing to do with anything but I liked the feeling in the dream. I liked feeling my arms full.

BILL

HAT And I know this is not what we – it's too soon – it's not practical. But I think I want it. I also know this is a massive bombshell and you don't have to answer right away it's fine if you just want to not say anything at all right now/

BILL /You want to keep it.

HAT Her.

Pause.

BILL I – good. Good.

HAT Good?

BILL Good. Her?

HAT I obviously don't know yet but I have a feeling it's a her.

BILL Great. Her. Excellent.

HAT I know we'd talked about – that this was something we wanted, maybe, at some point, way in the future, and I know it's not ideal timing – or even close – but – I think this could work.

Pause.

BILL Okay. Alright. Excellent. Okay.

HAT Say some other words. It sounds like you're being sarcastic.

BILL I'm not being sarcastic. I'm never sarcastic. You know that.

Pause.

Why don't I move in?

HAT What?

BILL Why don't I move in?

HAT With me? Move in with me?

BILL Yes with you! With you both!

HAT Is that what you want?

BILL Yes.

HAT Seriously?

BILL Yes.

Pause.

HAT Are you sure – it's so quick—

BILL Who cares? People spend too long faffing around in life before getting to the good bits.

HAT You think this is going to be a good bit?

BILL What do you think?

HAT *considers, nods.* BILL *kisses her.*

I can't believe this is happening.

HAT Me neither.

BILL We should tell your dad. Let's go and tell him now.

HAT Absolutely not. Are you mad.

BILL Right. Sorry you're right. I just – I want to tell them all. I want to shout it.

Pause.

HAT Let's just sit for a minute. Can we?

BILL Course.

They sit in the grass, basking in the moment. It's lovely.

11. Yoga Instructor

The actor playing **SILVERTONGUE** *is a* **YOGA INSTRUCTOR** *holding two rolled-up mats and wearing expensive-looking workout gear.* **HAT** *enters, visibly pregnant, bleary-eyed, and does a doubletake.*

YOGA INSTRUCTOR You did say eight, didn't you.

HAT Oh – yeah just – did you ring the bell, or—

YOGA INSTRUCTOR Door was open. The Practice teaches us never to turn away from an open door.

The **YOGA INSTRUCTOR** *rolls out* **HAT**'s *mat and then her own.* **HAT**'s *staring at her.*

HAT Are you a hairdresser?

YOGA INSTRUCTOR No?

HAT I mean, on the side. You don't cut hair on the side.

YOGA INSTRUCTOR I run a hugely successful yoga studio. I manage a teaching staff of fifteen. I wouldn't have that kind of time.

HAT Oh. Of course. Sorry. You look – exactly like my hairdresser.

YOGA INSTRUCTOR Must have one of those faces.

HAT That must be it.

Pause.

YOGA INSTRUCTOR Let's start with some reflection, shall we?

She sits cross-legged on her mat. She taps the other mat. **HAT** *tentatively follows suit.*

So. Hat. Can you tell me what you'd like to unlock in the next hour?

HAT I'd like to be different. I'd like to be a new me.

Pause.

That's what you guys do, right? That's what it said on the brochure.

Pause.

YOGA INSTRUCTOR The Practice can help you to grow and change, like water falling on a flower. But you have to turn your face towards the sky and say, hello rain.

HAT Okay.

YOGA INSTRUCTOR The Practice can help you be your best you, but only if you know that you are already good enough.

HAT I...

YOGA INSTRUCTOR You know that, don't you?

HAT looks at her. For a second, she almost might cry. The YOGA INSTRUCTOR presses her hands together as if in prayer.

Let's begin.

HAT follows suit. She inhales deeply.

12. Salt

Tipperary, 1895.

Water boiling on the stove. MICHAEL's *reading the paper.* BRIDGET *comes in, just out of bed.*

BRIDGET Morning.

BRIDGET *busies herself at the stove.*

How did you sleep? I had the most lovely dream.

MICHAEL I met Father Ryan this morning in the village.

BRIDGET Oh?

Pause.

MICHAEL He says he saw you out walking.

BRIDGET I didn't see him.

MICHAEL He says he saw you walking through the fairy fort.

The kettle whistles as it comes to the boil.

BRIDGET Spying, was he.

MICHAEL He was concerned.

BRIDGET Well tell him thanks for his concern but he can keep it for those that need it.

MICHAEL *smashes his fist on the table.*

MICHAEL What were you doing there?

BRIDGET Just walking. I told you.

MICHAEL You promised me.

BRIDGET

MICHAEL We agreed, didn't we, we agreed when we took this house that we'd leave them alone, and hope they would leave us in peace too. Our own little kingdom.

BRIDGET I'm sorry.

MICHAEL I couldn't bear to lose this, Bridget. Promise me you won't walk there again?

Pause.

BRIDGET I promise.

He reaches into his pocket and presses something into her hand. She looks at it. It's salt. **MICHAEL** *solemnly throws some over his shoulder.* **BRIDGET** *follows suit. He moves towards the door and starts to line the threshold with salt, slowly, ritually.* **BRIDGET** *moves towards the window and looks out.*

It's funny how it only looks like some stones in a circle.

13. Jug

Morning. **BRIDGET** *stands looking out at the fort.* **HAT** *sits with her hands around her knees.*

BILL Where were you?

HAT

BILL Where the *fuck* were you?

HAT I went for a walk.

BILL You can't do this to me.

HAT Do what?

BILL Leave like that. Turn off your phone. I was worried sick.

HAT I didn't ask you to worry about me.

BILL I thought you'd had an accident.

HAT We're separate people. We're not joined at the hip I'm not on the end of a piece of string looped round your finger.

BILL You've got our baby in there!

HAT Oh, so *that's* why you care so much.

BILL Don't be ridiculous, it's just an extra reason, it's not the reason – so you walked. You walked – all night.

HAT Mostly. I went to an internet café for a bit. Got some tea. Watched people Skype their loved ones.

Pause.

BILL Anything could've happened. You realise that. You could have been mugged or stabbed or raped or murdered. You could have become a statistic/

HAT /The city at night is so beautiful.

BILL You realise how inconsiderate, how selfish/

HAT /I pay my taxes. This is my city to walk in at night if I want to.

BILL You have to call me, at least. If you're not coming home I need you to call me.

Pause.

Hat—

HAT I'm tired, Bill.

BILL *(more gently)* Talk to me.

Pause.

Please.

HAT I don't know what to say.

Pause.

BILL Tell me something.

Pause.

HAT Sometimes I—

Pause.

Often I think that – people pour things into me – thoughts, feelings, love, rivers and rivers of it – and I hold those things, I hold all that like – a jug, I hold it all but can't – feel it. I'm – just, sort of a bit, hollow.

Pause.

Like if you've ever had hollow legs when you were nervous or scared. Like that but it's all of me.

Pause.

You could knock on my skin.

Pause.

BILL I don't know what to say.

Pause.

HAT You don't have to say anything.

Pause.

BILL So what you're telling me is – you feel like a jug.

HAT Yes, well, not *literally*—

BILL What kind of jug?

HAT What? Why does that matter?

BILL I'm trying to understand. Okay? Help me understand.

HAT Sort of like – a big water jug. The water sloshes around inside but it never stays for long.

Pause.

Does that make any sense?

BILL How can I help? Just tell me.

HAT I don't know.

Pause.

I'm sorry.

BILL It's okay.

BILL *tries to hold her.*

I love you.

She lets him, for a moment.

14. Silk

Tipperary, 1895.

Evening. BRIDGET *is holding a measuring tape. She's got a magazine open and is looking at a dress pattern and measuring her waist, her hips, the length of her arms.* MICHAEL *is trying to talk to her.*

MICHAEL You made a show of me today, Bridget. Everyone was asking after your health and me telling lie after lie.

BRIDGET I didn't ask you to lie.

MICHAEL And what else could I say? My wife is too good for us? My wife would rather stay home swanning about with bits of frilly lace than come to her nephew's christening? My wife would rather be alone?

Pause.

BRIDGET It's not lace, actually. It's silk. What do you think?

She shows him the image she's working from.

Silk's amazing. All that shimmer grows inside the belly of a worm. Can you imagine.

MICHAEL Mary said to tell you you're welcome to come and visit, see the baby, any time. They've called him Thomas. *(pause)* She asked why we'd none. Said it might settle you, to have something to do. I said it wasn't for want of trying. *(pause)* Is it.

BRIDGET I love this blue. I could make you a handkerchief, to match.

Pause.

MICHAEL Have you been at home all evening?

BRIDGET In this very spot.

MICHAEL Is that right.

BRIDGET Well, where else would I be?

Pause.

MICHAEL It's late. Come in to bed.

BRIDGET No.

MICHAEL *goes.* **BRIDGET** *turns back to her sewing.*

15. Shards

BILL *has cooked for* **HAT**. *It smells delicious. Just after* **JOY** *is born.*

HAT Do you think we'll manage this?

BILL It is quite a lot of food.

HAT Yes.

BILL You need it though. You pushed a human out of you the other day.

HAT Yeah.

BILL Well done.

HAT Thank you.

BILL No I mean it, you were amazing, watching you do that, the superhuman strength it must have taken I'll – never forget that.

HAT I don't think I could have done it without you.

BILL That's just not true though is it. I've never felt so useless in my life as I did in that room.

HAT I couldn't have done it without you there with me.

BILL Seriously?

HAT You've got a very calming face, did you know that.

BILL Thanks.

HAT Like the pool in the morning with no swimmers in it yet.

Pause.

Bill?

15. SHARDS

BILL Mmm?

HAT Do you think we'll manage this?

BILL I'd probably go for seconds—

HAT The baby. What if I can't manage the baby?

BILL Course you can—

HAT *(quietly)* I'm scared of her.

BILL Why?

HAT What if I break her?

Pause.

Drop her. I could drop her, so easily, she could just slip between my fingers like, like buttery toast, or an egg, or something and—

BILL You're not going to drop her.

HAT How do you know? You don't know that for sure.

Pause.

I'll drop her. I'll drop her on her head and she'll be hurt.

Pause.

BILL You could practise holding other things if you like, first.

HAT What?

BILL Well, I was scared, you know, of being responsible for a tiny breakable human, I think that's quite normal, I mean it's certainly normal to feel that according to the books I've read.

HAT *(touched)* You've been reading books?

BILL Of course. Then – well, I thought I'd practice, you know, on other things, so I started with a cushion cos that's sort of baby-shaped—

HAT Cushion won't smash. Anyone can hold a cushion.

BILL *picks up a cushion from the couch. Hands it to her. She takes it. Cradles it.*

This is easy-peasy.

She squeezes it quite hard.

BILL Congratulations! You have completed Level One.

BILL *takes it from her.*

So then – well, I bought this porcelain tea set and I've been practising with it.

HAT What?

BILL I started with a cup, then a cup and saucer, then I added the sugar bowl and one of those small jugs, you know, as my confidence grew.

HAT The milk jug.

BILL Is that a specific type of jug?

HAT Yeah.

BILL I can pretty much hold the whole set in my arms now, teapot and all, without dropping any of it.

HAT You can?

BILL I think you should try it. It really helped me. Wait a second, okay?

He jumps up, exits. BILL *returns holding a porcelain teapot, cup, saucer and jug. He holds out the teapot.*

Take it.

HAT *hesitates.*

HAT I feel silly.

BILL Go on.

HAT *stands up and gingerly takes the teapot. Holds it like a baby.* BILL *watches proudly.*

15. SHARDS

HAT *(tentative)* This is okay.

BILL Course it is—

HAT I think I like this.

She relaxes, rocks the teapot back and forth a bit.

I like this.

BILL Told you.

He passes her the cup as well. She cradles it, talks to it.

HAT I'm your mama. I'm your mama!

BILL *is beaming. He passes her a saucer. She coos at the china, her face relaxing.*

Yes I am. Yes I am.

Elated, **BILL** *adds the jug – but she isn't ready for it. All of the china falls and shatters, spreading shards across the floor.*

Pause.

(upset) I'm sorry.

Pause.

BILL We'd better get this cleaned up, don't want the baby to crawl over it.

HAT She's two weeks old. She can't even hold up her own head.

BILL Still, the shards could seep into the air and she could breathe them in, can't be too careful.

He starts to sweep. **HAT** *stands helplessly among the broken pieces.*

You'll get there. It's the most natural thing in the world.

He exits, carrying a dustpan full of porcelain. **HAT** *is alone.*

16. Make You an Offer You Can't

SILVERTONGUE *is sitting on the couch. Enter* **HAT**, *with shopping bags and pushing the buggy,* **JOY** *asleep inside.*

SILVERTONGUE Oh good. You're home.

HAT *drops all of her shopping.*

HAT *(calling out)* Bill?

SILVERTONGUE I let myself in, I hope you don't mind.

HAT *looks.*

HAT Kathy? Kathy from More Yoga?

Pause.

I didn't book a lesson. I don't think I did, I wouldn't've, booked one –

Pause.

Shit, or did I, on the app, by accident, maybe I sat on my phone and you've come all the way from Stoke Newington just because I sat on my – I'm sorry but now is not really a good t/

SILVERTONGUE /Why don't you sit down, Hat?

She stares at **SILVERTONGUE**, *alarmed.*

HAT *(calling out again)* Bill?

SILVERTONGUE He's not here. There's no one here. You're alone.

HAT I'm alone. I'm alone?

SILVERTONGUE Well. Not entirely.

16. MAKE YOU AN OFFER YOU CAN'T

She gestures into the buggy.

HAT Sorry. Who are you?

SILVERTONGUE I'm a shapeshifter.

Pause.

HAT I'm an admin assistant.

SILVERTONGUE Good for you. I have no fixed form.

Pause.

HAT What.

SILVERTONGUE I can assume the form of anyone I choose.

HAT Is that... I mean. Convenient?

SILVERTONGUE It is a boon. Must be shit, to be stuck in your skin.

SILVERTONGUE *seems pretty ensconced in the couch.* HAT*'s at a loss.*

HAT Well, since you seem to be staying – can I – get you anything?

SILVERTONGUE I would like a mani-pedi.

HAT I meant like, a drink.

SILVERTONGUE Pina colada.

HAT Tea?

SILVERTONGUE Irn-Bru.

HAT I've got tea or coffee. Or water.

SILVERTONGUE I'm not thirsty.

HAT Right. Okay.

Pause. SILVERTONGUE *gets up and looks into the buggy.*

SILVERTONGUE They're beautiful, aren't they, when they sleep. Like snowfall.

HAT Is there something you want?

SILVERTONGUE Me? No.

HAT Whatever it is, just spit it out. I'm tired. I want to sleep. I just want to sleep.

SILVERTONGUE I've come to make you an offer.

HAT I don't need anything, thanks.

SILVERTONGUE Wrong.

Pause.

You'd like to disappear.

Pause.

You don't have to pretend, Hat. It's just you here.

Pause.

I can help you disappear.

Pause. **HAT** *is listening intently.*

You won't cause a fuss. There'll be no search parties sent looking for you. No one will even notice. It will seem, from the outside, that you are still here.

Pause.

Are you interested?

Pause.

HAT No.

Pause.

SILVERTONGUE Well. Alright then.

SILVERTONGUE *makes as if to gather her things and go.*

HAT But if...

> **SILVERTONGUE** *stops*.
>
> If I was. Interested. Hypothetically.

SILVERTONGUE Hypothetically.

HAT How would it work?

SILVERTONGUE It's a bit like cloning.

HAT Sounds very – science-fiction-y.

SILVERTONGUE But it's not really like cloning. Listen carefully.

> *Pause.*
>
> Say the word, and I will change into you. I will put you on as if you were an evening dress laid out on my bed and I will wear you well. I will look like you and sound like you and do all the things you do. But I won't be you. I won't have all the stuff inside that you have. Inside I'll be hollow. So I'll have to be careful to keep everyone at arm's length, because if I let them get too close, they might see that you are missing. Especially people who love you. People who love you are much harder to fool.
>
> *Pause.*

HAT Let me get this straight – so – you. Would become me. You'd look just like me and sound just like me.

SILVERTONGUE That's right.

HAT And where would I go?

SILVERTONGUE Anywhere you wanted.

> *Pause.*

HAT Anywhere?

SILVERTONGUE Complete freedom. Like a balloon untied from a string.

> *Pause.*

HAT Somewhere really small.

SILVERTONGUE You could be in a speck of dust. Or – the static on a door handle on a hot day. Fizzing on someone's palm. Or a grape. Anywhere.

HAT And you'd do this, for me?

SILVERTONGUE Well, there is a cost. There's no such thing as a free – this.

HAT I could get you money.

SILVERTONGUE Money is no use to me.

HAT What then?

SILVERTONGUE The baby.

Pause.

HAT No.

SILVERTONGUE That is my price.

HAT Something else.

SILVERTONGUE This is how it works. You can't take her with you. When you go, if you go, you'd leave everything else behind. I'd be here. She'd be mine. My human child. I'd raise her. I'd love her.

HAT I love her.

SILVERTONGUE You don't.

Pause.

Don't deny it.

Pause.

HAT You should go. Bill will be home soon.

SILVERTONGUE Don't deny it. I know you. You think you're safe under your covering of skin? Might as well be glass.

16. MAKE YOU AN OFFER YOU CAN'T

Pause.

HAT Get out.

> **SILVERTONGUE** *gets up and looks in to the buggy.*

Get out get out get out get out get out!

> **SILVERTONGUE** *shrugs.*

SILVERTONGUE You've heard my offer. Take it. Or leave it.

> **SILVERTONGUE** *goes. From the buggy,* **JOY** *wakes and starts to cry.*

17. Floor

Tipperary, 1895.

BRIDGET's *sitting on the kitchen floor. She can't seem to move.* **MICHAEL** *enters.*

MICHAEL Bridget?

BRIDGET *doesn't look at him. Doesn't even hear him.*

Bridget!

She responds slowly, like she's underwater.

BRIDGET Yes?

MICHAEL Get up off that floor.

She doesn't move.

Get up. Come on now.

Pause.

BRIDGET *(soft)* Can't.

He looks at her, knotting his brow. He goes. She hugs her knees.

Too heavy.

18. The Happiest Human That Has Ever Lived

> **BRIDGET** *stays sitting on the floor throughout this scene.*
>
> **JOY** *is wailing.* **HAT** *is finishing up feeding her and rocking her back and forth. She is exhausted.* **BILL** *enters, holding a copy of "The No-Cry Sleep Method".*

BILL I've put your dinner in the microwave.

HAT What's the point? As soon as I sit down she'll—

> *Wailing increases.*

BILL I thought there might be something in here—

> **BILL** *holds out the book.*

HAT Right well I don't actually have time to read a whole book right now if you hadn't noticed.

BILL Alright, I'm only trying to—

> **HAT** *is almost crying with exhaustion.*

I'll skim it.

> *He starts to frantically leaf through the book.*

HAT I can't remember the last time I had a shower.

BILL There must be something in here—

HAT Or drank a whole cup of tea.

BILL I wish I could be home with you all the time.

HAT I'll do your job alright will we swop? I'll dress up as you and go to the office and you can do this you can stay here all day every day with her—

BILL Okay – I've found it – "Newborn Babies and Sleep".

He reads.

"There is little you can do to stop your baby from sleeping and waking up whenever they feel like it" …well that can't be right?

He turns over the page.

I'll read it on the Tube tomorrow. There must be answers in here somewhere.

HAT Do you think.

HAT *paces with baby, still wailing.*

BILL I feel useless. What can I do?

HAT Tell me something.

BILL Like what?

HAT Anything at all. Talk to me about any topic at all that two adults can talk about.

BILL Okay – eh –

Pause.

On my lunch break I bit into a fake sandwich.

HAT What?

BILL Yeah, the guys decided it would be funny to swop my sandwich for this extremely realistic rubber sandwich, I mean honestly, it was so lifelike, it looked completely real? And they'd wrapped it in the cling film that had had my original sandwich in it, so it sort of still smelled of ham—

Pause. He's chuckling to himself.

I can show you a picture—

HAT That's okay.

Pause.

BILL Oh – your mum rang earlier.

HAT Oh yeah?

BILL Said she couldn't get through to you?

HAT Why didn't you put her on?

BILL You were napping. I didn't want to wake you.

HAT I would have murdered you.

BILL That's what I thought.

HAT What did she say?

BILL They've booked to come over at the end of the month.

HAT They always do that, just book, and don't check if we're—

BILL And she asked about Sarah?

HAT Oh yeah?

BILL She's moved over here. Did you know?

HAT No, I. No.

The baby starts to quiet down.

BILL Few months ago. Your mum said she's split up with Kieran, after – well what happened.

HAT She's been here – for months?

BILL Since August. Working in a bar and living in some awful flat in Leyton, apparently.

HAT Sarah's working in a *bar*? Really?

BILL Your mum said she won't come home. Claire said she thinks Sarah's punishing herself.

HAT I had no idea.

BILL She gave me her address. Sounds like we should – I mean might be nice to – reach out, send a card or—

HAT Yeah. Yeah.

The baby has fallen asleep. **HAT** *looks at her, overwhelmed, wonderous. They whisper the next lines.*

BILL Maybe we could take the baby to see her.

HAT Who?

BILL Sarah?

HAT Oh. Yeah. We should.

HAT *is transfixed by the sleeping baby.*

BILL I'll heat your dinner up again.

HAT I'll be in in a minute.

BILL *goes.* **HAT** *picks the baby up, very carefully.* **BILL** *re-enters at some stage during the following speech.*

I want you to be the happiest human that has ever lived. Happier than a clam who's won the lottery. Happier than all the Oscar-winners in the world combined. I want to fill your head up with sunshine. I want to buy you a castle full of ice cream. I want to build you a boat and sail you beyond the horizon. You'll be happier than someone who has no regrets. Happier than someone who has never cried.

Pause.

I'll keep you safe always, my little one. I'll hold you so so tight. So tight and I won't let go or I could drop you, could drop you and break you break you break you/

BILL /Hat?

HAT *is trembling.*

HAT

BILL I'll take her.

HAT *doesn't move.*

Give her to me.

18. THE HAPPIEST HUMAN THAT HAS EVER LIVED

HAT *doesn't move.*

Hat?

HAT *passes the baby to* **BILL**.

What's wrong? What on earth is wrong?

HAT

BILL Tell me. Tell me and we will fix it.

HAT

BILL I'm taking her.

> **BILL** *cradles her and exits.* **HAT** *slides onto the floor in the same pose as* **BRIDGET**.
>
> **SILVERTONGUE** *appears.*

SILVERTONGUE Wouldn't you rather be a sliver of the wind.

Pause.

Or a bird feather. An apple core. A tree root. A double yellow line. A cockroach. An ant. A neon sign. A table leg. Lint in the pocket of a stranger. A bristle on a toothbrush. Rain. The crackle in the radio. An inhale. The ink in the last word of someone's favourite book. A dancing bit of light. A dancing leg. A tapping foot.

HAT What else?

SILVERTONGUE A silicon cell in a solar panel, making light and heat. A line of code. Dust in a hoover. A coffee bean. The glimmer of broken glass. The faded bit of an old poster. The chain on someone's front door. The numbers on the electric meter. The subject heading of an email. The credits at the end when everyone is leaving. The glitch in a skipping CD. The curl of a wave before it breaks. The peel of an orange. A wine stain on a glass. The crease in a napkin. The bit of a song that makes a heart skip. A stalactite.

HAT Put me in a grain of salt.

Pause.

SILVERTONGUE You know where to find me.

She goes.

19. Not Yourself

Tipperary, 1895.

MICHAEL comes home to find BRIDGET in exactly the same position, sitting on the floor. He goes to her. He blesses himself and shakes her.

MICHAEL Bridget—

BRIDGET I'm alright.

He hoists her up.

MICHAEL You're not yourself.

Pause.

BRIDGET What else could I be.

MICHAEL Let's get you up off the floor.

Pause.

BRIDGET I could be a silkworm. I could be so small and simple and useful.

MICHAEL Let's get you to bed.

BRIDGET I am tired. I'm really tired.

MICHAEL I'll send for Dr Crean.

BRIDGET Whatever you think is best.

20. Gone

>**BILL** *enters.* **HAT** *is sitting, wearing the coat she was wearing in Scene One. She is preternaturally calm.*

BILL You alright?

HAT Yeah.

BILL What're you doing?

HAT Sitting.

BILL Sitting's not an activity.

HAT It is.

BILL Like, just sitting staring into space is not an activity.

HAT I'm being present.

BILL Okay.

HAT Sit with me.

>*He sits.*

>Nice, isn't it?

>*Pause.*

BILL Joy go down okay?

HAT *(casual)* She's not here.

>*Pause.*

BILL What?

HAT She's at Sarah's.

BILL Sarah's? Why's she at Sarah's?

HAT I gave her to Sarah.

Pause.

BILL Okay, what are you talking about.

HAT I just need some space from her for a bit.

BILL That's why I'm here! I can take care of her!

HAT I need a break from her and it's better that she's there and not here. I need you to trust me on that one.

BILL A break.

HAT Please don't.

BILL You need a break, from our daughter.

HAT I can't actually have this conversation I am just about managing to sit here upright in this spot.

She quivers.

I thought—

BILL What?

HAT I thought she'd be better off with Sarah for a mum.

BILL *softens.*

BILL Look I know it's been – well, not like either of us expected, has it, it's been really hard, but this is madness, Hat. She doesn't even know Sarah very well –

HAT She's two months old. She doesn't know anyone very well.

BILL Why didn't you tell me?

HAT I'm telling you now.

BILL Why didn't you ask me, Hat?

HAT She's my child.

BILL Our child! For fuck's sake!

HAT She didn't come out of you.

BILL Well sorry for not having a womb!

HAT Don't be fucking petty.

Pause.

BILL Why are you being like this?

HAT Like what?

BILL Cruel. This isn't you. You're not cruel.

HAT Isn't this me? How do you know?

BILL I know you.

HAT Do you?

BILL Course I do, I love you!

Pause.

HAT That's what makes me think you don't know me.

He tries to touch her. She won't let him.

I thought—

BILL What?

HAT I thought I'd feel. Lighter.

Pause.

I don't.

Pause.

BILL *(very tender)* Why don't we go and get her?

HAT We can't.

BILL Hat.

HAT I gave her to Sarah. I told you.

BILL

HAT Sarah's sorting it all out. She's a lawyer. Did you know that? She's a really hotshot lawyer actually. She was with Arthur Cox.

20. GONE

Pause.

BILL Okay. Here's what's going to happen. Me and you, we'll put on our coats and our shoes and we'll go to Sarah's and pick her up and bring her home. And then we'll talk about how we're going to deal with this. We'll get you help. There's people who can help.

HAT I didn't bother to take off my coat.

BILL Half the battle.

Pause.

What do you think?

HAT Whatever you think is best.

BILL *heaves a sigh of relief.*

BILL It will be alright, Hat, I promise you.

HAT *nods.*

I'm just going to go and get my coat. Alright? You put on your shoes and then we'll go.

HAT *nods again.*

We can do this. You just need to talk to me. Keep talking to me. About everything. Okay?

HAT *nods a third time.* **BILL** *kisses her and she lets him and for a moment it's like rain in a drought.*

Stay right here. I'll be right back.

HAT Okay.

He exits. **HAT** *reaches down and slowly puts on her shoes. She stands up. She looks in the direction* **BILL** *has just exited. She slips out.* **BILL** *re-enters with his coat on.*

BILL Hat?

21. Faith

Tipperary, 1895.

A low fire is glowing in the hearth. **BRIDGET** *is standing at the sink. She's wearing small gold earrings from this point until the end. The glint of them is friendly. She plunges her hands into the water.* **MICHAEL** *enters, his coat on.*

MICHAEL Bridget?

She jolts at his voice, caught unawares.

You're up?

She starts to wring out the shirt she's washing, squeezing the water from each sleeve.

I met the doctor coming down the path.

BRIDGET He's just gone.

MICHAEL Why are you up?

BRIDGET I'm a little better.

MICHAEL I shouldn't have left you. You should be resting.

BRIDGET I felt like doing a bit of washing.

MICHAEL You should be in bed. You're in no state to do anything.

Pause.

I went to see Father Ryan. He's coming now to pray with you. It could be our last hope, to bring you back to yourself.

BRIDGET Alright, Michael.

MICHAEL Go and rest.

BRIDGET I'm nearly finished here.

MICHAEL Where did you get those?

He gestures to the earrings.

BRIDGET They were my mother's.

MICHAEL Why are you wearing those now? Are you going somewhere?

BRIDGET No.

MICHAEL Are you expecting someone?

BRIDGET I felt like a little shine.

She goes, taking the wet washing with her. He stares at her like she is a stranger.

22. Insides

A park bench. HAT *waits.* SILVERTONGUE *appears from between the slats of the bench. They sit for a moment without speaking. Then –*

HAT I've been thinking.

SILVERTONGUE I told you my price.

Pause.

HAT You'd raise her?

SILVERTONGUE I'd teach her everything I know.

HAT You'd love her?

SILVERTONGUE Obsessively.

HAT Always?

SILVERTONGUE For eternity. I'd never leave her side.

HAT And she'd be safe. You'd keep her safe.

SILVERTONGUE I'd let no one come near her. No one would touch her. Ever. I'd make sure of it.

Pause.

HAT Would it hurt?

SILVERTONGUE Not at all.

HAT Would it take long?

SILVERTONGUE Blink of an eye.

Pause.

All you have to do. Is bring her to me. And it's done.

23. Michael Is Worried

MICHAEL sits at the table. In his hands is a blue silk handkerchief, which he is twisting and weaving through his fingers anxiously. He stands, thinking someone's at the door. It's just the wind. He sits again. Another sound. He twitches. BRIDGET *calls, from offstage.*

BRIDGET *(offstage)* Michael?

MICHAEL Yes?

BRIDGET Water, please.

MICHAEL Coming.

He gets up and fills a glass at the tap, leaving the handkerchief on the table. He lets it overflow. He pours some away into the sink. He puts the glass down on the table. He completely forgets the task he's in the middle of. He picks up the handkerchief again and sort of stands there holding it for quite a while.

BRIDGET Michael?

She is standing there behind him.

MICHAEL I said I was coming.

He holds out the water. She takes it and drinks deep. She indicates the handkerchief.

BRIDGET I'm glad you like it. It reminded me of your eyes.

A moment. Then she goes. MICHAEL *puts the handkerchief in his pocket.*

24. Nesting

SARAH*'s in her flat. There is new baby stuff everywhere.* JOY *is in her arms, clasped like precious treasure. The pram from Scene One is on the stage.* SARAH *is still wearing her coat from Scene One.*

SARAH Right.

Long pause.

You're so small. Aren't you?

Pause. The baby is awake, but not crying. Small noises.

I should take off my coat.

She doesn't. She sits, gazing at JOY. *She does this for a long time. Her eyes never leave the baby's face. Gradually the baby noises stop as* JOY *falls asleep.* SARAH *doesn't move until an urban noise from outside – a distant siren, or a shout in the street perhaps – brings her back into the room.*

Right.

Pause.

Let's put you in your cot.

She gets up. Goes off. She comes back without JOY. *She takes off her coat. She sits down again. She doesn't know what to do with herself. She goes off again to check the baby. A thunderous banging on her front door.*

BILL *(offstage)* Sarah?

SARAH *comes back in.*

SARAH Who's that? Stop shouting—

BILL It's Bill.

SARAH It's one in the morning—

BILL Let me in, would you—

> BILL *bursts frantically into the room.*

Where's Joy?

SARAH She's asleep, through there – what are you doing here, it's late—

BILL Is Hat here?

SARAH No—

BILL She's disappeared.

SARAH What?

BILL Not answering her phone—

SARAH Well when did you last see her?

BILL About two hours ago.

SARAH Well. Two hours hardly constitutes/

BILL /We were supposed to come here. I thought she might have come here.

SARAH She hasn't.

> *Pause.*

She's done this before, hasn't she, gone for a bit always comes back. She likes her space, always has since we were children.

BILL This is different.

> BILL *moves towards where* JOY *is sleeping.*

SARAH I just put her down to sleep, don't wake her—

BILL I've come to take her home.

SARAH Oh?

BILL "Oh", she says. Fucking "Oh". All sweetness and innocence.

Beat.

SARAH Look, can this conversation wait 'til morning—

BILL No! No it can't. I'm taking her home.

SARAH Hat wants her here. With me.

BILL Hat doesn't know what she wants right now. Trust me.

SARAH Why should I?

BILL What?

SARAH Trust you?

BILL What did Hat tell you? What did she say?

Pause.

SARAH She said you thought this was best.

BILL And you believed that?

SARAH I didn't know what to believe.

Pause.

I still don't.

BILL What's that supposed to mean?

SARAH She said she wanted to keep the baby safe. Wouldn't say much more than that. So I thought she meant. Safe from you.

BILL From *me*?!

She stares him down.

SARAH She was so frantic and I thought maybe she was, embarrassed, to tell me what was really going on but - at the end of the day, she's family, she needed me and I - I didn't ask that many questions.

BILL I cannot believe what I'm

SARAH No offence, alright, but I don't know you! I've met you once! How am I to know what kind of man you are.

BILL This is completely

SARAH How am I supposed to know if she's safe with you? For all I know, you two could've split up and now you're just some guy who's come barging into my place in the middle of the night.

Pause.

BILL This is ridiculous. I'm her father.

SARAH She needs love. Babies die, without love, did you know that/

BILL /I'm her father and I'm taking her home.

BILL *stands up and moves towards the exit to where* JOY *is sleeping.* SARAH *blocks his way.*

During the below, a scuffling noise is heard, off, and the sound of footsteps, which SARAH *and* BILL *don't notice.*

Get out of the way, Sarah.

SARAH Can't.

BILL Get out. Of my way.

SARAH I'll call the police. Say you broke in.

BILL You wouldn't dare—

SARAH Try me.

BILL Call them! Go on! I'll say you've kidnapped my daughter, BECAUSE THAT IS THE TRUTH

SARAH You call them then.

BILL I will.

SARAH Use my phone, I've got unlimited UK minutes, go ahead, who do you think they'll believe?

BILL You wouldn't—

SARAH FUCKING TRY ME

Hold. Like she might deck him. And then **SARAH** *suddenly seems to crumple.*

Just wait 'til morning. Let her sleep here. Just for tonight. Please.

BILL *goes off to get the baby.*

BILL *(offstage)* Why's the window open in here?

SARAH What?

SARAH *rushes offstage—*

BILL *(offstage)* She's not she's not in the cot – where is she she's not

SARAH *(offstage)* Joy? She was just – I just checked her – Joy oh my God—

25. The Burning

Tipperary, 1895.

The hearth is lit. It crackles and spits. **BRIDGET** *and* **MICHAEL** *are standing, bodies close. Strange charge. Like they might punch each other, or have sex, at any minute.*

BRIDGET Why're they all here?

MICHAEL I asked them to come.

BRIDGET I don't want them all here in our house.

MICHAEL They want to talk to you. Help you. There are things that can be done to help you.

BRIDGET I need rest. I need space. That's all.

MICHAEL They're worried about you. They want to get a look at you.

BRIDGET Tell them to go. Please.

MICHAEL Why? Do you have something to hide?

BRIDGET I just want to be alone with you.

MICHAEL How about you tell me something.

BRIDGET Anything.

MICHAEL Just one question.

BRIDGET Anything.

MICHAEL Where's Bridget Cleary?

BRIDGET What are you talking about?

MICHAEL Where's my wife? Ever since she went walking in that fairy fort she's not been right. You've taken her, piece by piece and now you have her. Where is she? Where is she?

BRIDGET *almost smiles.*

BRIDGET Michael. This is madness.

MICHAEL Do you think I'm stupid? Is that it?

BRIDGET Michael. You can't seriously/

MICHAEL /You think you can just pull the wool over just like that? You think you can look at me like that and I'll fall at your feet?

BRIDGET Michael.

She holds his face in her hands.

Remember that day we went swimming in the river? October and raining and just because we wanted to. Told no one. Saw no one else all day. Might have been that everyone else died. We wouldn't have known. It's only us in the world that were there that day. Only us.

He looks at her, long and hard.

Forget about everyone else. It's me.

MICHAEL And who's that, when she's at home.

Pause.

You think you can fool me. You're just a stranger in her skin.

He grabs her roughly by the shoulders, lifts her off her feet and starts to shake her. One of her gold earrings falls out onto the floor.

(shouting, to the room) You'll all see. You will soon see her go up the chimney!

26. Really You

BILL *waits at their flat. He waits and waits, restless and angry and fearful. His phone rings and he leaps to answer it –*

BILL Sarah. No. She's not rung you either? Yes the police said to call them as soon as she makes contact so if she – yeah. I can't believe she would but – the woman I spoke to said they can't rule anything out at this point. Yeah. Okay I'm going to go in case she's trying to call. Okay. Yeah. Bye. Bye.

BILL *hangs up. He is exhausted, a wreck. He waits and waits. And waits. We begin to think this is how the play ends.*

Suddenly, **HAT** *enters the room, very quietly. Baby* **JOY** *is in her arms. It's morning by now and a shaft of bright morning light comes skittering into the room.* **BILL** *is momentarily blinded.*

Hat is that you?

He squints at her.

Hat? Oh my God you

HAT Hi.

He takes her in.

BILL Oh my God.

HAT I'm so sorry I I'm so sorry

She holds out the baby, who is making small sleepy noises. **BILL** *takes her, drinks her in.*

BILL Oh my God. Oh my God.

He looks at **HAT**.

I can't believe it, Hat.

He looks at her long and hard. She holds his face in her hands.

HAT

BILL I can't believe it's really you.

HAT *doesn't say anything. She is bathed in light. A tear rolls down her cheek.*

End of Play

PROPS SETTING LIST

STAGE RIGHT
BILL's Samsung mobile phone (charged)
SARAH's iPhone (charged)
pint of lager
glass of orange juice
Sweet Aftons
matches
carved wood for whittling
pocketknife
sewing kit with:
measuring tape
needle and thread
gold fabric
dressmaker's shears
glass of wine
washing up basin
tea set (teapot, pre-cracked milk jug, sugar bowl, cup and saucer) on tray
dustpan and brush
No Cry Sleep Solution book
blue silk handkerchief
Bucket for porcelain

ONSTAGE
DSL:
Mirror
Chair
door closed
KY on floor for cigarette extinguish

CSR:
sofa (L-R)
pram facing SR with baby face down & brakes off

DSR:
fire extinguisher on wall
door fully open

CS:
small round table with:
tea light on
ashtray with KY
salt in bowl
folding chairs SL and SR of table (SL face DS, SR on angle)
phone on wall
patio doors closed with locks all open
Curtain Open
Plant SR of door

PATIO USR:
barbecue with 2 x Tools on onstage arm, "meat" and flame paste
Smoke machine connected to barbecue
2 x pink garden chairs
dead plants in pots US
2 x glasses near tap upside down
2 x glasses spare hidden in patio
Mic set & path to spikes clear
Path to tap clear
Matches w/3 ready set in pot SR of chair

BOG USL:
deckchair
cassette player
mic on stand

STAGE LEFT
sun reflector
sunglasses
practical tape recorder
pack of cigarettes and lighter
HAT's Samsung mobile phone (charged)
two coffees in white mugs (one with tons of whipped cream)
glass of wine
wooden board with canapés (3 x sausage rolls and olives)
wide-toothed comb
hairdresser's magazines
yellow floral quilt with blue silk, two dress design books
cushion
crossword/word search book and pencil

BILL's bag
washing up basin with ladies' blouse and water
ashtray with KY
Matches set in QC w/3 ready

SOUND/EFFECTS

The light sound of rain (p16)
BRIDGET stands in the rain (p17)
The sloshing sound of the dishwasher is like the sea (p21)
Water boiling on the stove (p31)
The kettle whistles as it comes to the boil (p31)
Joy wakes and starts to cry (p47)
Wailing increases (p49)
...still wailing (p50)
The baby starts to quieten down (p51)
A low fire is glowing in the hearth (p60)
The baby is awake, but not crying. Small noises (p64)
Gradually the baby noises stop (p64)
Urban noise from outside (p64)
A thunderous banging on the front door (p64)
A scuffling noise is heard, off, and the sound of footsteps (p67)
The hearth is lit. It crackles and spits (p69)
His phone rings (p71)
Small, sleepy noises (p71)

LIGHTING

A shaft of bright morning light comes skittering into the room (p71)
She is bathed in light (p72)

THIS IS NOT THE END

**Visit samuelfrench.co.uk
and discover the best
theatre bookshop
on the internet**

A vast range of plays
Acting and theatre books
Gifts

samuelfrench.co.uk
samuelfrenchltd
samuel french uk

www.ingramcontent.com/pod-product-compliance
Ingram Content Group UK Ltd.
Pitfield, Milton Keynes, MK11 3LW, UK
UKHW021844210426
5322IPUK00022B/462